ISRAEL

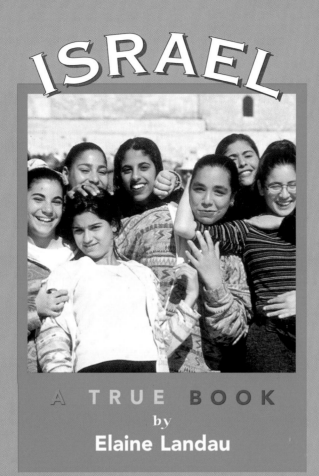

A TRUE BOOK

by

Elaine Landau

Children's Press®

A Division of Grolier Publishing

New York London Hong Kong Sydney
Danbury, Connecticut

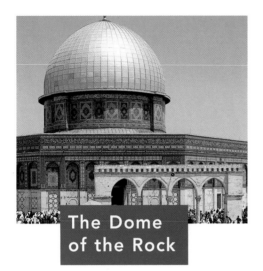

The Dome
of the Rock

Reading Consultant
Linda Cornwell
*Coordinator of School Quality
and Professional Improvement
Indiana State Teachers
Association*

Author's Dedication
For Brenna Joy Tudor

Visit Children's Press® on the
Internet at:
http://publishing.grolier.com

Library of Congress Cataloging-in-Publication Data

Landau, Elaine.
Israel / by Elaine Landau.
      p.   cm. — (A True book)
   Includes index.
   Summary: Surveys the history, government, people, culture, and
economy of Israel.
   ISBN: 0-516-20983-3 (lib. bdg.)   0-516-26765-5 (pbk.)
1. Israel—Juvenile literature. [1. Israel.] I. Title.
DS118.L319   1999
956.94—dc21   98-41192
                                                          CIP
                                                          AC

GROLIER
PUBLISHING

Contents

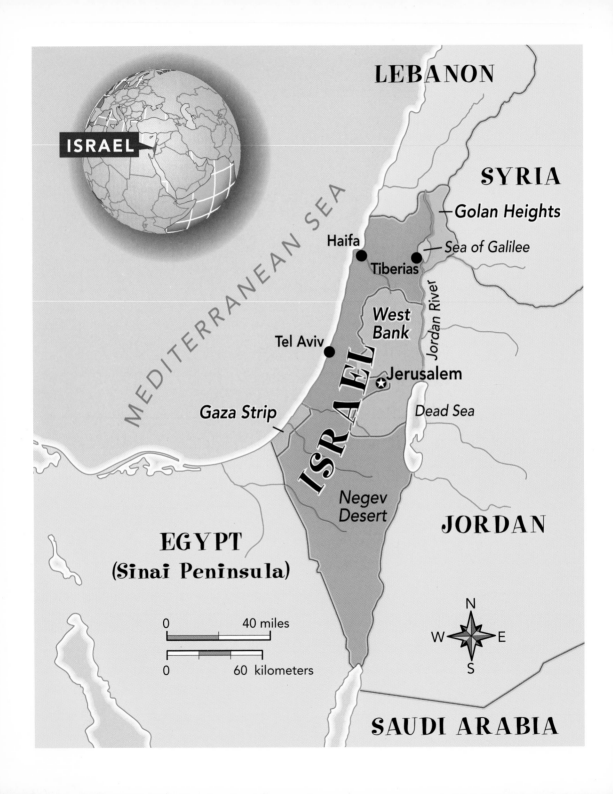

LEBANON

SYRIA

ISRAEL

—Golan Heights

—Sea of Galilee

MEDITERRANEAN SEA

Haifa

Tiberias

West
Bank

Jordan River

Tel Aviv

Jerusalem

Gaza Strip

Dead Sea

ISRAEL

Negev
Desert

JORDAN

EGYPT
(Sinai Peninsula)

0   40 miles

0   60 kilometers

N
W   E
S

SAUDI ARABIA

A Jewish Homeland

Israel lies on a narrow stretch of land on the eastern shore of the Mediterranean Sea. At first it may seem out of place in the Middle East. But it has a special reason for being there. Although bordered by Arab countries such as Syria, Lebanon, Jordan, and Egypt, it is a Jewish homeland.

Israel is small in size—just 10,840 square miles (28,000 square kilometers). Its landscape is quite varied. Within

Israel's western border is on the Mediterranean Sea (left). The Negev Desert (below) is Israel's driest region.

its borders are mountains, deserts, seacoasts, and valleys.

Israel is varied in other ways as well. It offers an unusual blend of the ancient and modern. Historical sites and religious shrines exist near scenic beaches and busy cities.

The Israeli Flag

Israel's flag features the Star of David, an ancient Jewish symbol. The colors of the flag are the same colors as a *tallit*, a prayer shawl.

When Jews pray, many wear a blue-and-white-colored prayer shawl called a *tallit*.

From Past to Present

To understand Israel today, it is important to know its history. Jews first lived in the region during biblical times. But through the years, as various foreign conquerors invaded the area, large numbers of Jews were forced to leave. By the late 1800s, most of the

The land of Israel is important to the history of Jews, Arabs, and Christians.

people living in the area, which was called Palestine, were Arab. Meanwhile, in Europe a Zionist movement toward establishing the land of Israel as a Jewish homeland had begun to grow. The goal behind this movement was to create a place where Jews would always be welcomed and protected.

But as large numbers of Jews arrived in Palestine, Arabs began to resent them. Tensions ran high. In November 1947,

In this 1948 photograph, a Jewish immigrant family arrives in Israel to begin a new life.

This photograph, taken on July 2, 1948, shows soldiers of the newly formed Israel.

the United Nations tried to ease the tensions. It called for a division of the land into separate Jewish and Arab nations. In May 1948, the independent country of Israel was officially born.

However, the Arabs refused to accept the Jewish

homeland. Within twenty-four hours the united armies of Egypt, Jordan, Syria, Lebanon, and Iraq attacked the new nation. But Israel survived. By 1949, it had defeated the Arab forces as well as added some of the land set aside for a new Arab state to its own boundaries.

About 150,000 Arabs were already living in the newly acquired territory. They were angry that a separate place for Palestinian Arabs had not been created. Now they had to adjust to being a minority in a Jewish homeland. However, the Israelis insisted that they had to hold on to the seized area to defend against future Arab attacks.

A 1948–49 struggle known as the War for Independence

Israeli soldiers on the move during the 1948–49 War for Independence

Captured Egyptian soldiers in a truck (right) are transported past Israeli soldiers who are on their way to fight other Arab forces during the Six-Day War.

began a series of conflicts that continued through the years. Although many thought Israel would never survive an ongoing Arab attack, it did. And in the Six-Day War of June 1967, Israel seized additional Arab territories. They included the

Sinai Peninsula, Golan Heights, Gaza Strip, and the West Bank.

Israel controlled an area where more than one million Arab Palestinians already lived. As a result, the bitter feelings increased. Later peace agreements required Israeli troops eventually to begin leaving the controlled regions. Still, not everyone was pleased with this requirement.

Some Israelis insisted that they should not have to return

In 1993, Israeli Prime Minister Rabin (left) and PLO Chairman Arafat (right) signed a peace agreement. (U.S. President Clinton stands in the center.) But the difficult relationship between Israelis and Arabs continues.

territory that was important for Israel's defense. Peace efforts were also made more difficult by the Palestine Liberation Organization (PLO). The PLO consists of a number of united Palestinian Arab groups who want to create a separate Palestine. The PLO and other similar groups launched terror-ist attacks mostly against Israeli civilian, or non-military, targets. In return, Israel struck PLO-held areas in surrounding Arab nations. As a result, the peace process has been put on hold many times. And Israel must constantly be ready for more military action.

The Israeli People

Israel has a population of about six million people. Although they come from various parts of the world, most of its residents are Jewish. Recently, thousands of Jews from both the former Soviet Union and Ethiopia have settled in Israel. With people from so many different places,

Israel's population is made up of people from many racial, ethnic, and cultural backgrounds.

it's easy to see racial, ethnic, and cultural differences among Israeli Jews. Yet as Jews, they have a common spiritual bond.

Other people living in Israel include Muslims, Druze, and Christians. There are many

Palestinians who remained after their territory became part of Israel. Arabs in Israel do not always get along well with the Jewish majority. The Palestinians often have complained of inferior schools, housing, and job choices.

Many Palestinian schools have crowded classrooms where students have few materials and supplies.

גן העצמאות
حديقة الاستقلال
INDEPENDENCE
PARK

This road sign is written in Hebrew (top), Arabic (middle), and English (bottom).

Tensions between the two groups have been worsened at times when Palestinians have openly sided with anti-Israeli groups.

Hebrew is Israel's official language. English is also spoken and is taught in schools. All Israeli street and road signs are written in Hebrew, Arabic, and English.

Most people in Israel live in the northern or central part of the nation. Most of them live in apartment buildings in cities. Jerusalem, Israel's capital, is its largest city. It is a holy place for Jews, as well as for Christians

A view of the capital city of Jerusalem, which includes both historic and large modern buildings

and Muslims. Tel Aviv, on Israel's Mediterranean coast, is the country's second-largest city. Only a small portion of the people live in the countryside.

Some people live in a collective community known as a kibbutz. Kibbutz members work, but they don't receive pay. Instead they are given food, housing, child care, medical services, and other necessities. In a kibbutz, everyone shares in the work, property, and profits.

Workers tend plants in the greenhouse of a kibbutz located in the Negev Desert.

Originally most kibbutzim were farming communities. But today many develop and run high-tech factories that produce a variety of products for sale to other countries.

No matter where they live, Israelis value education. There is free public education for everyone through grade twelve. There are also a number of colleges and universities for students who

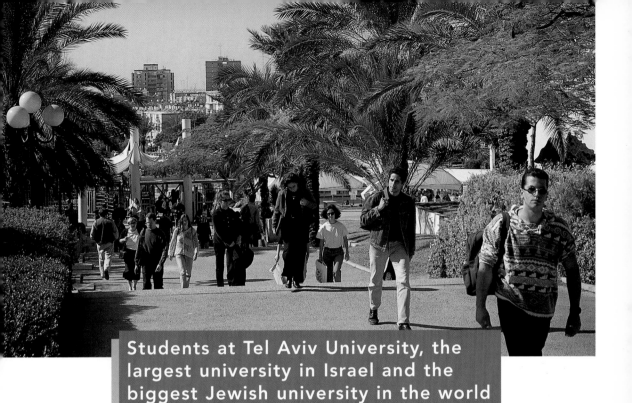

Students at Tel Aviv University, the largest university in Israel and the biggest Jewish university in the world

wish to continue their education. These include Haifa University, Hebrew University of Jerusalem, Tel Aviv University, and the Technion Israel Institute of Technology.

Beyond the Kibbutz

The first kibbutz, Dgania, was established in 1923. From Israel's early days, the kibbutz community provided Israel with a good way to work the land and to defend its borders. Many kibbutzim members have become top officers in the Israeli Defense Forces (IDF). Others are serving as government officials.

A kibbutz worker picks mangoes

One—or both—of these kibbutz members may someday become a government official or military officer.

Government

Like the United States, Israel is a democracy. Democracy is a way of governing in which the people choose their leaders in elections. Israel's lawmaking body is a parliament known as the Knesset. The country does not have a written constitution. It follows a set of basic laws established by the Knesset.

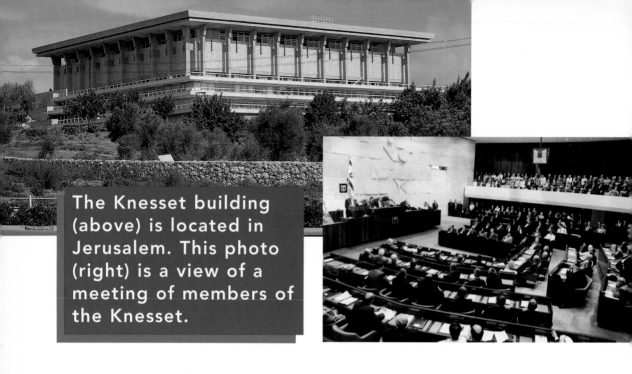

The Knesset building (above) is located in Jerusalem. This photo (right) is a view of a meeting of members of the Knesset.

Although Israel has a president, that person does not have a great deal of power. Instead, the Israeli prime minister acts very much as the U.S. president does.

Elections for the prime minister and Knesset are usually held at the same time. Just as

Almost all young Israeli men and women are required to serve in the country's military.

in the United States, Israelis can vote when they turn eighteen years old.

Israeli men and almost all Israeli women who are not married must enter the military when they turn eighteen. Men must serve for three years. Women are required to serve for two years.

The Economy

Israel is not rich in natural resources, such as coal, water, and natural gas. But many people there live comfortably. This is partly because a large number of its early inhabitants had valuable job skills that helped the country get start-ed. The Israelis also wisely

Farmland in the Negev Desert is possible because of a system of pipes that brings water to the area.

used whatever was available to them. They irrigated dry land for farming. They drained swamps when the land was needed for crops. Israel also has been fortunate to receive

The workers in this Israeli factory manufacture medicine and vitamins.

money and supplies from the United States and other countries.

Today, Israeli factories manufacture paper, plastics, scientific instruments, chemical products, packaged foods, clothing, and other items. Its farms produce fruits, vegetables, poultry, eggs, and grains. Underwater mining operations in the Dead Sea have yielded potash, salt, bromine, and magnesium. Copper, clay, and gypsum are also mined in the desert.

This salt mine is located near the Dead Sea.

This tour of Christians is visiting the site believed to be the burial place of Jesus.

Israel's economy depends heavily on tourism. Visitors enjoy the country's warm dry summers, which last from April to October. Winters in Israel are cool, but mild. Since the area is rich in biblical history, religious journeys to the region are popular.

In recent years, many fine restaurants have opened in Israel, to the delight of both residents and tourists. Like its

Customers at an outdoor restaurant in Jerusalem

Falafel (above) and borekas (right) are two traditional Middle Eastern foods served in Israel.

people, Israel's food is quite varied. Menus often reflect the different backgrounds of those living there.

Traditional Middle Eastern foods such as falafel (fried chickpea patties), *shawarma* (roasted lamb slices), and *borekas* (cheese- or potato-filled dough) are common. But European Jewish dishes including chicken soup and gefilte fish are readily available. (Gefilte fish is ground fish that is formed into balls or cakes and cooked in fish broth or baked in tomato sauce.)

Art and Culture

Israel is rich in art and culture. It has many museums and theaters. Israeli writers, painters, and sculptors have become well known through-out the world. Award-winning Israeli authors include Chaim Bialik, Amos Oz, and A. B. Yehoshua.

At times, Jewish themes are evident in the work of Israeli artists. Some of the most interesting works capture Israel's struggle for survival.

Frequent rehearsal sessions like this one have made the Israel Philharmonic Orchestra well known all over the world.

Music is another important part of Israel's heritage. The Israel Philharmonic Orchestra is respected throughout the world. There are many less well-known orchestras as well.

Israel's history is one of success in many areas of life—from its culture to its economy. Israeli leaders seek to find ways to end the fighting between Israel and the Arab countries in the region. Although a permanent peace agreement has not been reached, the Israelis want to continue to work toward one. They know that peace is important to the nation's future.

To Find Out More

Here are some additional resources to help you learn more about Israel:

 **Books**

Allard, Denise. **Israel.** Raintree Steck-Vaughn, 1997.

Bacon, Josephine. **Cooking the Israeli Way.** Lerner Publications, 1986.

Department of Geography. **Israel in Pictures.** Lerner Publications, 1992.

Haskins, James. **Count Your Way Through Israel.** Lerner Publications, 1992.

Stoppleman, Monica. **Jewish.** Children's Press, 1996.

Organizations and Online Sites

**America Israel
Friendship League**
134 East 39th Street
New York, NY 10016

**America-Israel
Cultural Foundation**
317 Madison Ave.,
Suite 1605
New York, NY 10017

Embassy of Israel
www.israelemb.org

This site contains information about Israel, including everything you need to know to plan a visit. There are links to current events, education, and government sites, as well.

Israel
www.Israel-UN.org

Here you'll find a list of Israel's ambassadors to the United Nations, information about the peace process between Israel and Arab countries, and maps that compare Israel's size to the size of other countries and to the state of California.

Important Words

irrigate to supply water to crops by artificial means, such as channels and pipes

landscape an area of land

majority more than half of a group of people of a particular race, ethnic group, or religion

minority a group of people of a particular race, ethnic group, or religion living among a larger group of a different race, ethnic group, or religion

potash a mixture of potassium salts that come from plant ashes

poultry birds such as chickens, turkeys, ducks, and geese

Zionist movement the movement to create a Jewish homeland in Zion, the land of Israel

Index

Meet the Author

Elaine Landau has a Bachelor of Arts degree in English and Journalism from New York University and a Masters degree in Library and Information Science from Pratt Institute. She has worked as a newspaper reporter, children's book editor, and a youth services librarian, but especially enjoys writing for young people.

Ms. Landau has written more than one hundred nonfiction books on various topics. She lives in Miami, Florida, with her husband Norman and son, Michael.